Emotional Engulfment

Jay Harris

Presentation by *BookLeaf Publishing*

Web: www.bookleafpub.com

E-mail: info@bookleafpub.com

ISBN: 9789357440875

First edition 2023

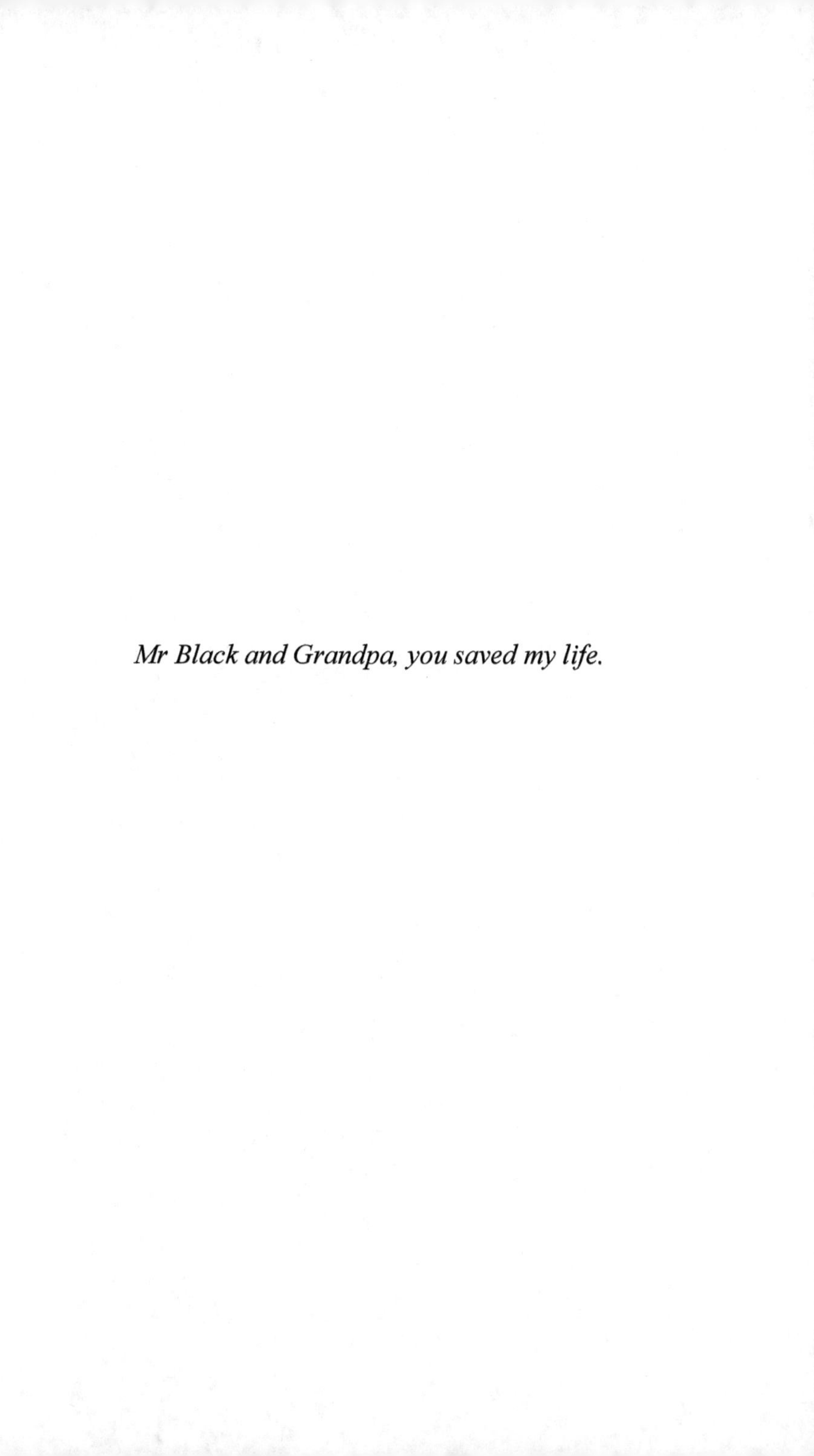

Mr Black and Grandpa, you saved my life.

ACKNOWLEDGEMENT

Friends and family, thank you.

Sunrise

He was her sunrise
He brought life to her eyes
Golden rays of love surrounding them
Til dusk settled upon them.
Twilight shrouded their passion
And the sunset fell upon their joy
And the dark of night extinguished their love
Scattered amongst the stars.
That's where you'll find it
Their broken love
Still shining bright
Only seen at night.
When you look up you'll see it
Their love
Their loss
Their eternal regret.

Reflect

Looking upon the past
It stains
Being present
Tears at the soul
The future
The freedom
Worth the
Late night tears
Every screaming moment
Moments that haunt
That beckon
Through the stain of time calling
The call left unanswered
As if the tears were worth it all
All the freedom
The future has it
It's been sought after
Begged for
Now here
Here is the freedom
At all cost.

Tears

Tears fall as the memories pass by
The heart is hurting wondering why
Why it couldn't work
Why was love left to die
The lingering questions hurt the heart
Why such hands fell apart
Apart from lives combined
Apart from broken hearts
There is no answer
Not a new one
Not one
That hasn't been muttered
Been muted
Been ignored
Or screamed aloud
In the darkest night
Haunting one's thoughts
But loneliness abounds
Broken
Battered
Lovers
Their ghost of them
Them haunting
Each other
Is still just a ghost.

Behind

For so long I laid there
Bare upon the stone
Left broken
Battered
The world saw all
Stagnant
A shattered heart
Barely a shadow
Of oneself
Left alone
Lying there
Losing faith
Facing storms
Of screaming
Of rage
Emotions let loose
Reality
A downpour
Drowning
Spiraling down
Left lying
Broken
Upon the shore
Left behind
Lost.

Enchantment

The world
So wonderous
Like love
Miracles occuring
Yet loss
Is there
Both stacked
Up upon each other
They block the view
Of what's wrong
None seeing through
The blinding of both
Are encompassing
Denying the changes
Lost by the wayside
No magic
Between those seeking
Those lost
Yet there in the cracks
There is love
The miracle
The once upon a time
A storm of love
Loss
And the magic in between.

Clouds

Looming just ahead
The sky darkens
Dimming of the day
A sign of rebirth
Yet still such death
It haunts
Blanketing the world
Surrounding the broken hearted
Leaving them in the dark
Lonely once more
Lost
Even as dawn beckons
And a new day appears
But still that small chance
A new change
A wondrous life looming
Reminders of such glory
Pulled tight
Ropes fraying
Clinging to a dream
Once terrible
Once supreme
Love and loss
Braided and twisting
One is in the distance

One is in sight
In a simple hands touch
But which one
Which daydream
What nightmare
Looms ahead
As eyes gaze up
Still wondering.

Raw

Torn apart
Memories they linger
Leaving a bad taste
On a lover's tongue
Just there
The residue of love
Barely a taste
Leaving as the begging words dry up
A haunting
A ghosts glow
The glow of love
It's there in the shadows
Leaving an imprint
Of a love lost.

Exhaustion Blues

My head falls to my chest,
My eyes they close in a blink,
All of me is exhausted,
I've got the exhausted woman's blues.

No idea what to do,
Oh wait I should probably sleep,
If I could sleep,
But I can't find it, sleep.

With no sleep and not enough coffee,
Not enough of anything,
No energy, no get up and go,
I've got the exhausted woman's blues.

I feel blue too,
Blue is an emotion,
Just a state of existence,
Just a chance to subsist on this, this life.

Just exhausted,
Always exhausted,
Blue too,
I've got the exhausted woman's blues.

Knowing better doesn't help,
Today I'm blue,
Tomorrow it's you,
We're all just exhausted, just blue.

We've all got it, the exhausted woman's blues.

Let

I let him have my body,
Afterwards he left me alone in bed,
He left alone with my memories,
My memories of our love torn asunder,
I let myself cry for what was and might have
been.

He had my interest from hello,
But later left me with barely a goodbye,
With a necklace of intention and tears falling he
was gone,
His best intentions left me broken, heart and soul
in pieces,
Saying goodbye to love had me saying hello
heartbreak.

Later I let him have my body again,
I had his interest one time more,
My memory should have been buried,
I couldn't bury my heart,
My soul shone for him.

Always,
I know better though,
Again,
I still want it,
Him.

Depression

Deep into depression,
Tears fall fast,
Regrets wreak havoc,
Dark in the night,
Demons well up,
From within the screams, oh the screams,
Standing on the edge,
The dreary depths call,
Onto the ledge,
The precipice looms,
I long to fall,
A steep drop,
Then nothing,
Nothing but peace,
God peace is...
Everything,
Everything I want,
Everything.

Lying

Does a predator change?
How can one love evil?
Does love cancel out hate?
Or does the tiger not change it's stripes?
The expectation is one,
But it becomes the other,
Fate is a bitch as they say,
What should one expect,
The time is full of evil,
The lies one tells themselves to excuse love,
Are they sad,
Or are they expected,
Is human will strong enough,
Strong enough to change evil's fate,
Love shouldn't fall by the wayside,
Will it win though,
That's the question,
Lying to yourself,
Doesn't win the fight,
Neither does love,
Or so says will,
Human will isn't enough,
It seems.

Long Time Ago

Death reaches out,
The shadow of love,
Just there,
Lingering,
A whisp,
Of emotions,
Of loss,
The love,
Is left behind,
A glance,
The love,
It's whispering,
Magical,
And fleeting,
Love,
It's still there,
In the heart left behind.

Left Behind

If wishes were granted,
You'd be here,
I'd be there,
In your arms,
In love,
Fate being kind,
That's not how the story goes,
We're separated now,
And then,
We couldn't work,
No matter the love between us,
The fates were not sweet,
And our love wasn't meant to be,
Yet I still wish for you,
Still long for you,
Years and lives apart,
You're still there,
Left behind in my memory.

Dreams

There's only one life,
One chance to live,
One chance to love,
And spending the time we have together,
With one another is a blessing,
Fates have blessed us with this,
This love once held impossible,
Never thought we'd have,
All of life changes in an instant,
And that moment we met,
We knew,
Then,
That'd we'd been given a gift,
That gift,
Our love,
Is worth,
All of life.

Longing

The day is chilled,
The heart is too,
As the seasons changed,
Love changed too,
It was lost,
As the leaves were dying,
So was romance,
Fate was splitting the difference,
Nothing told,
Nothing explained,
Just lost,
A phantom limb,
Still there,
Still longed for,
But lost,
Broken heart,
Broken promises,
Broken word,
Still,
It's longed for,
Over this loss,
Of oneself,
Of one's love.

Brighter

Future so bright,
Now broken,
The shards lying on the floor,
Reflecting the lies and loss,
Putting them back together,
Cuts to the quick,
Bones and blood exposed,
Bleeding,
Love falling from the vein,
From the eyes,
Future fallen apart,
The heart torn apart,
No repair,
Lies and falseness,
The cause,
The results,
Lying on the floor,
Torn apart,
Lost.

Divided

Choices were made,
Hearts meant to be together,
Broken,
Torn apart,
The fear,
It was the reason,
Or so the story went,
But it was just a story,
Fairytales are often just that,
A story told,
A lie spread,
Make believe,
Love stories,
Real life,
It changes the story,
Makes it real,
Breaks the heart,
Breaks apart,
The fairytale,
Meant to believe in.

Does It Get Better?

The roses don't make it better,
Thorns pricking thumbs,
Drips the blood,
On the tile floor,
The lies have blackened the love,
The love that was promised,
False words,
Broken promises,
The anger,
The rush,
The love is still begged for,
Why when it hurts,
Why,
Always asking why,
Why the pain,
The blood and pain,
Is it love,
If it makes you bleed,
Yet still together,
Broken,
And bleeding,
Screaming,
Crying,
But still,
Together.

Real Love

As I sit here growing cold,
Growing old,
I realize I love you,
I also,
Realize you can't love me,
Then my heart breaks,
Tears fall,
Reality interferes,
I am lost,
Lost in love with you,
I have no chance,
I have no choice,
I am still in love with you.

Cynical Love

Standing on a precipice,
I am dumbfounded,
In awe my soul,
Falling into the depths,
He calls for me.

Laying down I look up,
I am at a loss,
Words can't come to me,
Limbs unable to move,
Our eyes meet both teary.

Still my body frozen,
Neither of us reaching out,
My throat won't clear,
He sees me gasping,
He falls down, his knees hit ground.

Like my body his knees now dirty,
Through the tears life muddled, muddy,
Fingers, cold, outstretched,
Eyes still teary, two though cloudy,
That final gasp, a love so sad, incomplete.

Kaleidoscope

The thrill of our time together finds me firey red,
Running into his arms so strong turns my life
sunny yellow.
Seeing all those happy people made me green
with envy,
When I'm with him my life is a kaleidoscope of
pinks and purples,
Leaving me alone though he makes me blue,
My nights alone cause my outlook to be
blackened by doubt,
Love and lust blur together, my life is gray now,
I've embraced the gray,
Made friends,
Lovers even,
With the gray landscape that is my life.